A radar station.

Design	Cooper · West
Editor	James McCarter
Art Director	Charles Matheson
Researcher	Dee Robinson
Consultant	Tony Search
Illustrators	Rob Shone
	Elsa Godfrey

© Aladdin Books Ltd

Designed and produced by
Aladdin Books Ltd
70 Old Compton Street
London W1

Published in the USA in 1984 by
Franklin Watts
387 Park Avenue South
New York, NY 10016

Library of Congress
Catalog Card No 83-50851

ISBN 0-531-04724-5

Printed in Belgium

The Electronic Revolution

RADIO & RADAR

Frank Young

FRANKLIN WATTS
New York·London·Toronto·Sydney

Foreword

Radio technology was developed at the beginning of this century. For the first time people could communicate with one another over long distances instantly. Since then, radio systems have become far more sophisticated and have found many different applications in everyday life.

Using radio waves and satellites, we can telephone friends in different countries, and receive "live" television pictures from across the world. Radar systems guide international air traffic and help scientists discover more about our weather. As this book shows, radio and radar technology is one of the most important aspects of the electronic revolution.

TONY SEARCH: *Technical Consultant*

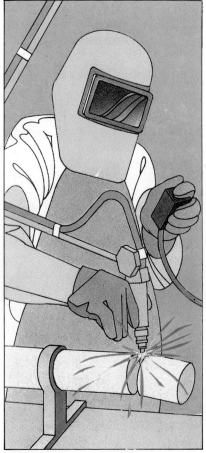

Lasers

Computers

TV and Video

Contents

Communication and control   8

Radio waves   10

Broadcasting and receiving   12

Radar systems   14

Under the sea   16

Keeping in touch   18

Radar and the weather   20

Tracking with radio   22

Radar defense   24

Radio from space   26

Glossary   28

Index   29

Radio and Radar

Satellites

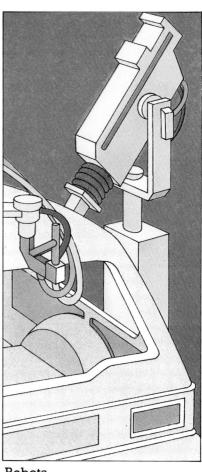

Robots

Communication and control

If you switch on your radio and turn the station dial backward and forward, you will hear a variety of broadcasts. There will be news and current affairs programs, sports reports, weather forecasts and music shows. But radio is not just important for public information and entertainment. Airline pilots use radios to keep in touch with air traffic control authorities; ambulance drivers can be guided quickly to the scene of an accident and the police can keep in touch with headquarters. Radio is the invisible communications link that the modern world depends upon in all sorts of ways.

▷ A radio link is essential in police work. Information or extra assistance can be called upon at any time.

▽ The hand-held control of a model aircraft is really a small radio transmitter. The model has an antenna to pick up the radio signals which control it.

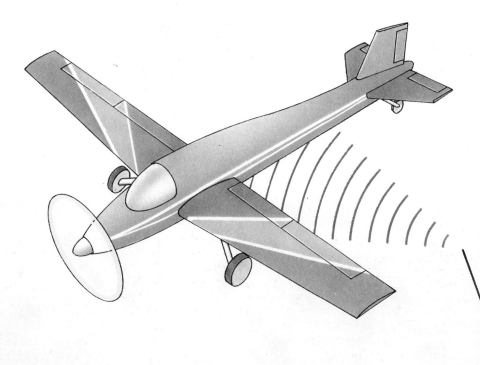

Remote control with radio

With radio, not only can we communicate over long distances — we can control things as well. Radio signals picked up by a model aircraft, for example, operate electronic equipment which controls the model's engine, rudder and wing flaps, to alter its speed and direction of flight.

Radio waves

Radio signals are a form of electrical energy that travels as waves through the air or through space, spreading out in all directions. You can think of them as being like the ripples in a pond when you throw a stone in it. Radio waves are created by changing currents of electricity. You may have noticed that if something like an electric drill is switched on when you are listening to the radio, you can hear a crackle of interference. This is because your radio has picked up the radio waves generated by the changing electric current in the motor of the drill.

Radio waves are usually transmitted from high towers. The waves can carry the information for TV images as well as for sound.

Frequency and wavelength

The distance between the two peaks of a radio wave is called the *wavelength*. The height of a peak is the wave's *amplitude*. The greater the amplitude is, the stronger the radio signal, but more power is needed to transmit it.

All radio waves travel at the same basic speed. But the wavelength changes as the frequency changes — the higher the frequency is, the smaller the wavelength becomes, as the three diagrams show.

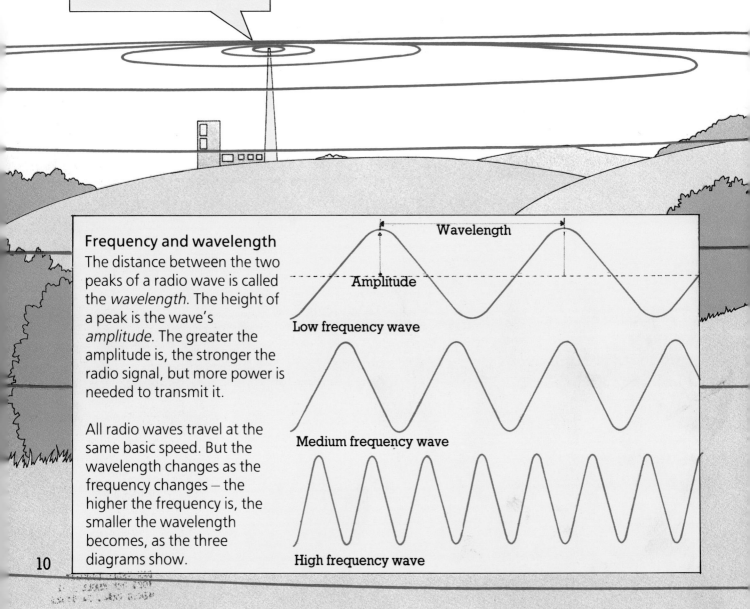

Wavelength

Amplitude

Low frequency wave

Medium frequency wave

High frequency wave

Different types of radio waves

Just as the ripples on a pond can be large or small, or closely packed together or spread out, so can radio waves. The number of complete waves that pass a given point in a second is called the *frequency* of the wave. Radio waves of different frequencies are used for different purposes. Low frequency waves (those in which there are comparatively few waves per second) are often used by shipping, because they tend not to be affected in poor weather conditions. Medium frequency waves are used for local broadcasting. Very high frequency waves are often used for TV broadcasts. Both the sound and pictures of a TV program are carried by these waves.

TV broadcasts are transmitted using very high frequency radio waves. The TV antenna picks up these waves and sends them to the TV set.

A radio's telescopic antenna picks up the radio waves transmitted from the radio station. Most portable radios also have another antenna contained within the set.

11

Broadcasting and receiving

The radio waves broadcast from a transmitter spread upward and outward in straight lines. But the surface of the Earth is curved, so how are people living on the other side of the world able to pick up the radio signals that we broadcast to them? And why don't the radio waves travel straight out into space? The answers lie in the Earth's upper atmosphere. At an approximate height of between 80 and 400 kilometers (50 to 250 miles) is a layer of atmosphere which contains electrically-charged particles. This layer is called the *ionosphere*, and the way that it affects radio waves allows us to broadcast around the world.

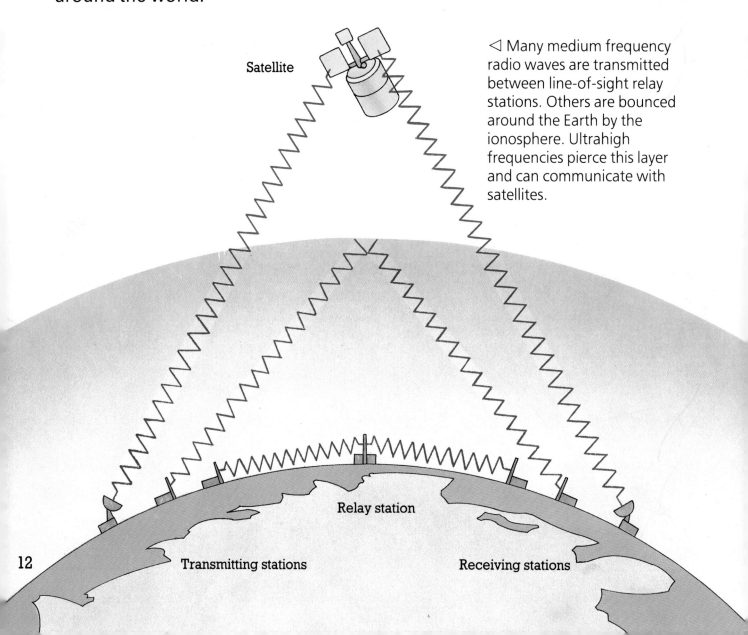

Satellite

◁ Many medium frequency radio waves are transmitted between line-of-sight relay stations. Others are bounced around the Earth by the ionosphere. Ultrahigh frequencies pierce this layer and can communicate with satellites.

Relay station

Transmitting stations

Receiving stations

Reflecting radio waves

The ionosphere causes radio waves to bend. The degree of bending depends upon the frequency of the wave: the lower the frequency, the greater the degree of bending. At the frequencies used for most radio broadcasts, the degree of bending is so great that the waves are reflected back to Earth. This allows us to communicate around the curvature of the Earth.

Ultrahigh frequencies and satellites

Ultrahigh frequencies are bent so little by the ionosphere that for practical purposes they pass straight through it. This means that they can be sent to satellites which can retransmit the signal back to Earth. Special dish-shaped antennae are used to concentrate and aim ultrahigh frequency radio waves at orbiting satellites.

▽ A dish antenna concentrates radio waves into a beam in the same way as the reflector on the rear of a bicycle lamp focuses a beam of light. Dishes are also used to pick up weak radio transmissions.

Radar systems

Radar systems are a specialized use of radio to detect objects and find their positions and distance. The word radar is short for "Radio Detection And Ranging." It works by sending out a series of ultrahigh frequency radio waves in short pulses. When the pulses hit an object, they are reflected back. The reflection is picked up by the same antenna and shown on a display screen as a bright spot, called a blip.

Reading a radar screen

Because radar works as well at night or in foggy conditions, it is an invaluable aid in ship and aircraft navigation. In addition to detecting other ships and aircraft, radar will pick up rain clouds, electrical storms, or a large flock of birds. A radar operator needs much experience before he can read just what his radar blip reveals.

▽ Shipping in busy sea routes, such as the English Channel, depends upon radar. The latest radar systems contain highly sophisticated electronic equipment. They are linked to a computer for an instant analysis of their readings.

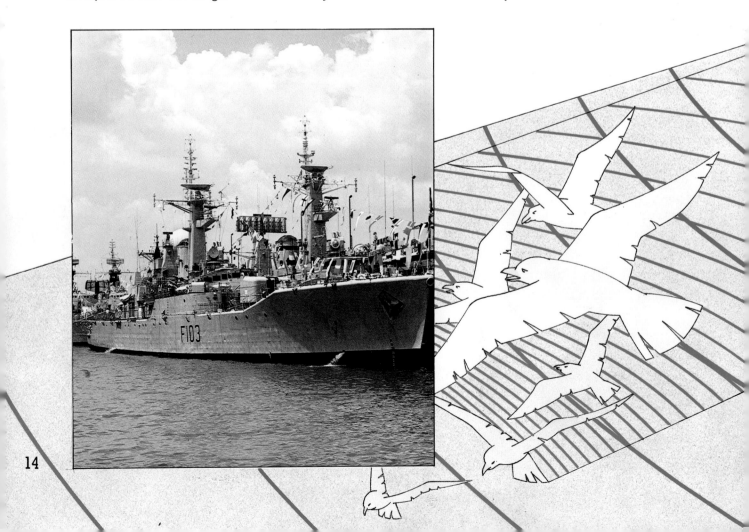

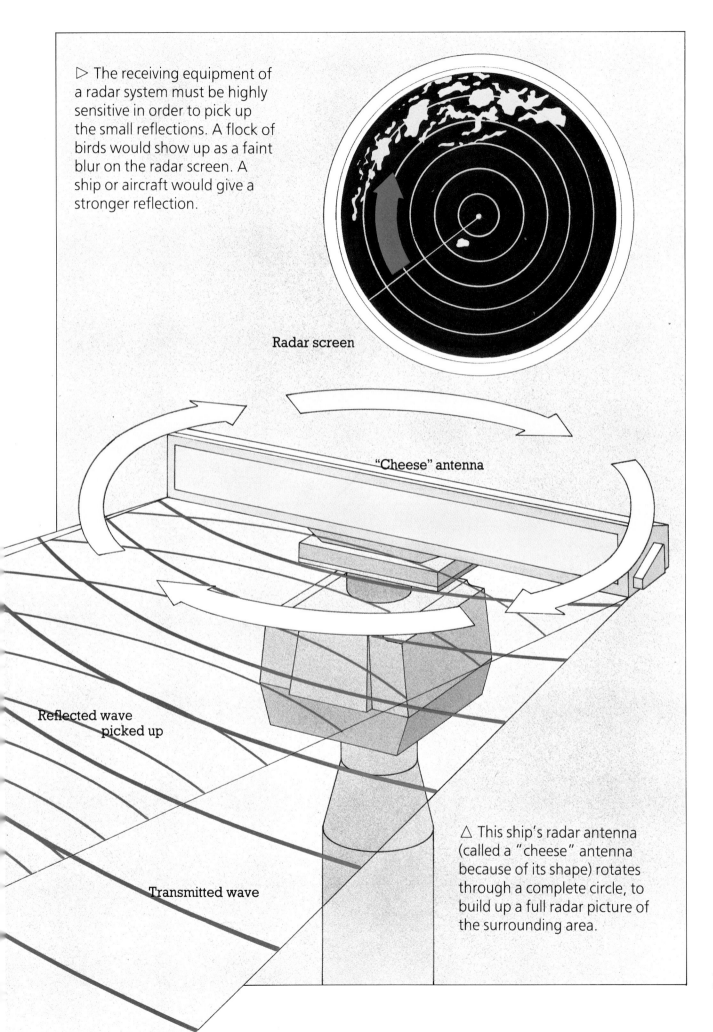

▷ The receiving equipment of a radar system must be highly sensitive in order to pick up the small reflections. A flock of birds would show up as a faint blur on the radar screen. A ship or aircraft would give a stronger reflection.

Radar screen

"Cheese" antenna

Reflected wave picked up

Transmitted wave

△ This ship's radar antenna (called a "cheese" antenna because of its shape) rotates through a complete circle, to build up a full radar picture of the surrounding area.

Under the sea

Radio waves are rapidly weakened when they pass through seawater, so radar systems cannot be used to explore the ocean depths. Instead, sonar systems are used. Sonar – short for "Sound Navigation And Ranging" – works in a similar way to radar. It transmits pulses of high-pitched sound waves and picks up the echo made when they reflect off underwater objects. Sound waves travel much further and faster through water than they do through the air.

▷ A modern fishing vessel no longer has to rely on its captain's judgement and experience. Sonar equipment can detect shoals of fish, so that the captain can be reasonably sure of making a catch.

Using sonar

Submarines use sonar to detect enemy surface ships and other submarines. But the submarine's sound signals may also be detected by enemy vessels. Sonar is also used to chart the varying depths of the ocean floor. This can be done by surface ships which have sonar equipment beneath their hull. The sonar echo is picked up by underwater microphones called hydrophones.

▽ Beneath the ocean, sonar acts as the ears and eyes of a submarine. The computerized sonar displays are found in the heart of the submarine's operations room.

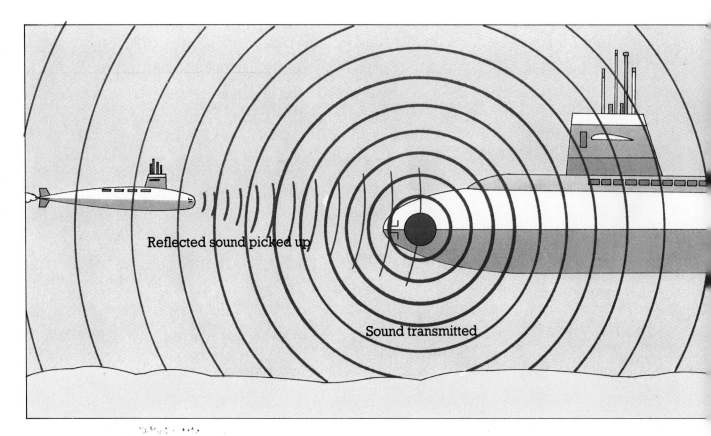

Reflected sound picked up

Sound transmitted

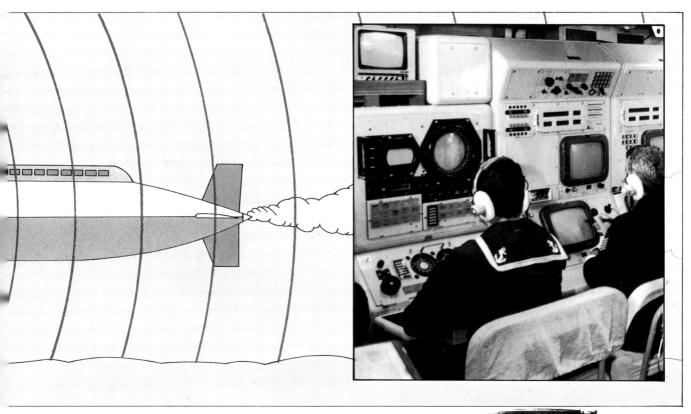

Keeping in touch

Since the early days of radio, enthusiastic amateur radio "hams" have communicated with one another worldwide using personal transmitters. But in the last ten years or so, the personal use of radio has grown remarkably. Portable two-way radios keep business people in touch with their offices and alert doctors to an emergency. Today millions of people use Citizen's Band, or CB, radio. CB radios are often fitted in cars and used to warn other users of any hazards on the road.

Avoiding interference

The increase in the use of radio has brought problems with it. So many broadcasts are made that they are beginning to interfere with one another – you can hear this on some of the frequencies on your own radio. There are strict regulations designed to stop unauthorized people from using frequencies that are reserved for emergency purposes, for example.

▽ "10-4 and adios big buddy!" CB was first used by truck drivers in the United States and has a language of its own. "10-4" means yes or message understood, "adios" is signing off and "big buddy" is just being friendly!

△ Good radio communications are vital to many forms of rescue work. These mountain rescuers can keep in touch with their base, which can tell the nearest hospital how badly the rescued climber is injured.

▷ Car telephones link into the national telephone system by radio. They work only within a certain distance from a major telephone exchange.

Radar and the weather

Most people find it useful to know what the weather is going to be like when they go out or plan a trip. But accurate weather forecasts can also help farmers to reduce crop damage or warn airports of approaching storms that could delay flights. At sea, an advance knowledge of weather conditions is essential – it could be the difference between life and death.

Short-term forecasts

Ground-based radar stations are used to detect and monitor belts of cloud or rain. The radar readings are analyzed by computer and displayed on a computer screen. In the most up-to-date systems, complete pictures of the current rainfall situation are available every 15 minutes. By seeing how the pictures change, the weather can be predicted with great accuracy for up to six hours in advance. Satellite photographs covering a wider area help meteorologists to see how the local conditions fit into the overall weather pattern.

▷ This radar map is of western England. It is built up from the readings from three ground stations and shows a belt of heavy rain approaching from the west.

▽ A network of radar stations is needed to cover a large area. The readings from each station are sent to the central meteorological office for computer analysis.

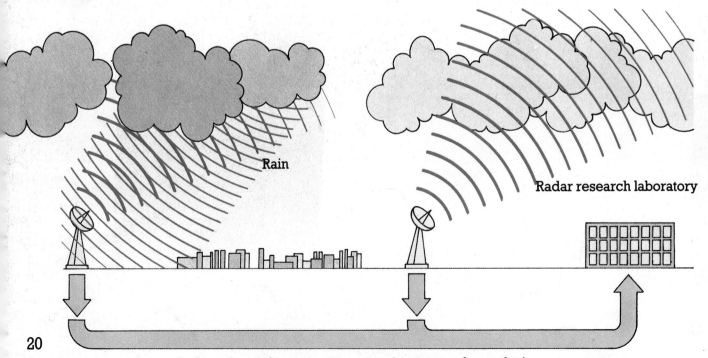

Rain

Radar research laboratory

Radar relays information to a central computer for analysis

Tracking with radio

Aircraft and ships use radio in a routine way for navigation and communication. But radio becomes vital when things go wrong – when a yachtsman's boat is damaged in a storm, for example. His survival equipment will include a small emergency radio "beacon," powered by battery. The beacon transmits a radio signal which can be picked up by the rescue services, even in poor weather conditions or total darkness.

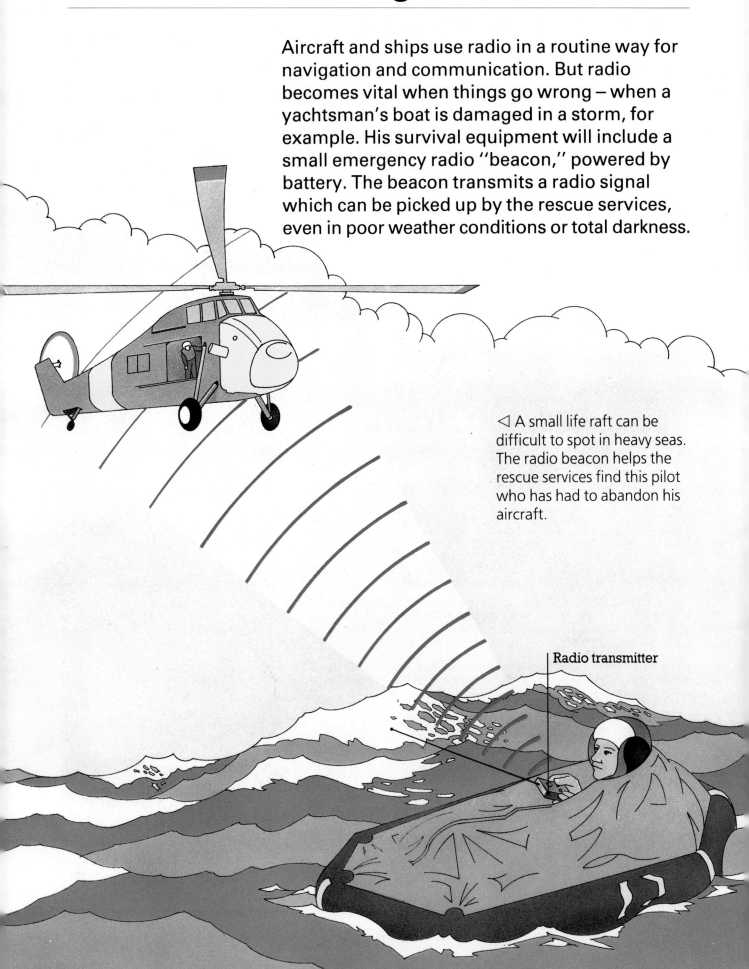

◁ A small life raft can be difficult to spot in heavy seas. The radio beacon helps the rescue services find this pilot who has had to abandon his aircraft.

Radio transmitter

Radio "bugs"

Most people have heard of radio "bugs" from spy films and police serials on television. The bug is a small radio transmitter that enables the police to secretly track the movement of a suspect's vehicle, for instance. Scientists use transmitter bugs to study the behavior of animals in the wild. The transmitter is attached to an animal, usually by means of a collar. The transmitters must be small and light, so that they don't bother the animal. In this way, a small team can track animal movements over a large area, day and night.

▽ This tiger has been shot with a drugged dart, to enable scientists to attach the radio collar. Tigers are becoming rare in the wild, and the knowledge that scientists gain using this method can help to protect those that remain.

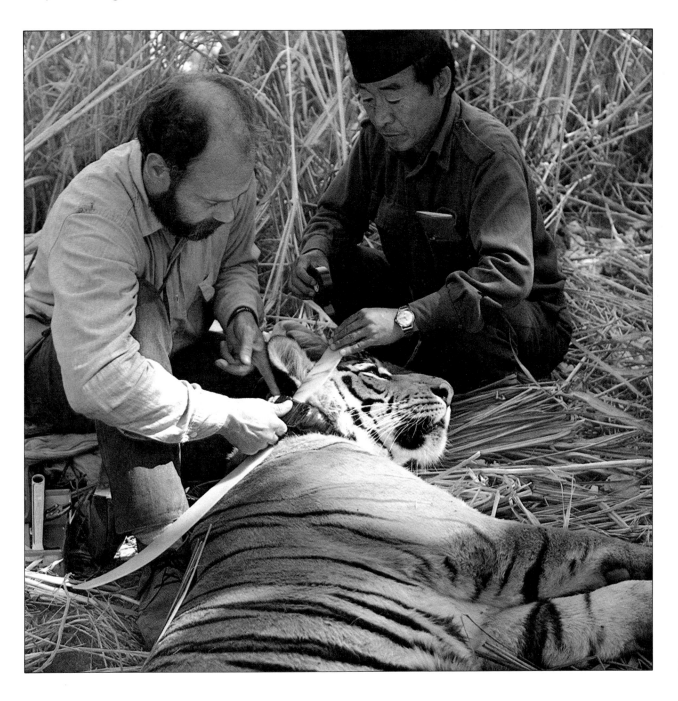

Radar defense

Armies have always depended on good communications, but in today's electronic age they are essential. Radar was first used by the British at the beginning of World War II (1939-45), to detect enemy fighters and bombers. Today's radar systems use computers to analyze their readings. They can not only tell the position and flight path of enemy planes or missiles, but also guide missiles to counter-attack them.

"Jamming" radio waves

By broadcasting and directing radio signals of the same frequency, it is possible to "jam" enemy radar and communications to prevent them from working properly. For this reason, armed forces keep the frequencies they use a closely guarded secret and continually change to new ones.

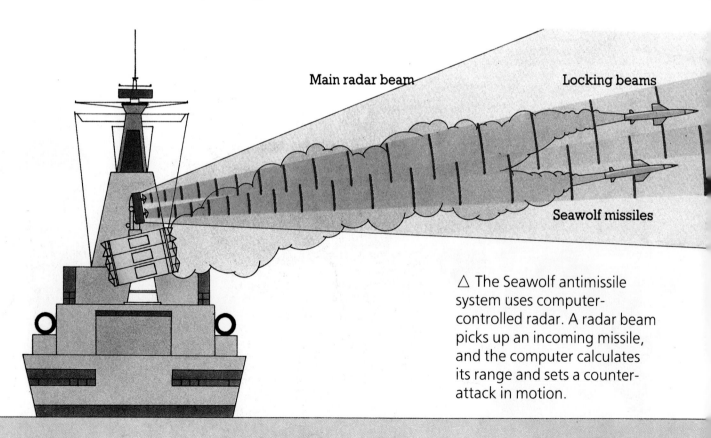

Main radar beam

Locking beams

Seawolf missiles

△ The Seawolf antimissile system uses computer-controlled radar. A radar beam picks up an incoming missile, and the computer calculates its range and sets a counter-attack in motion.

◁ This Boeing AWAC (Airborne Warning and Control System) carries powerful radar equipment in the mushroom-shaped dome on its fuselage. AWACs are maintained on 24-hour patrol, ready to detect enemy attack.

▽ The cockpit is also the communications center of a modern fighter. The pilot can keep in touch with other members of his squadron and with his ground base.

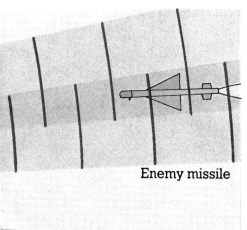

Enemy missile

A second radar beam is locked onto the target, and a Seawolf missile is automatically fired. The missile follows this second beam to the target. This system can destroy targets as small as a naval shell in supersonic flight.

Radio from space

As we have seen, radio and satellite technology are closely linked. The first communications satellite was launched in 1962. Using radio waves, the satellite could transmit pictures from one continent to another as they were filmed. Since then, the quality of satellite broadcasts has greatly improved. With the development of the space shuttle, we can now put satellites in orbit much more easily. One project planned for the shuttle is to launch three satellites that will allow communication with all parts of the Earth.

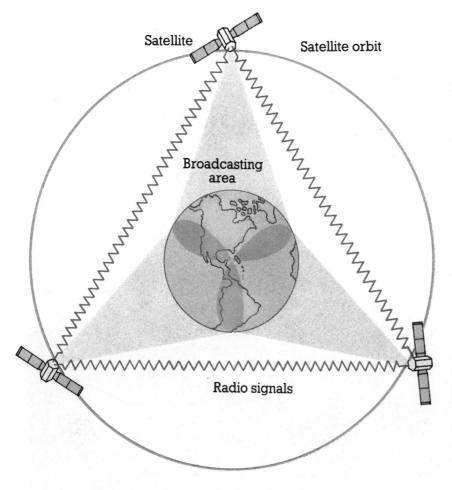

△ With just three satellites, it is possible to broadcast to every place on Earth. The satellites must orbit at a height of 36,800 km (23,000 miles). The satellites are launched by the space shuttle.

The satellites orbit at the same speed as the Earth rotates. This means that they always "see" the same part of the Earth. By sending radio signals from one satellite to another, the whole Earth can be covered.

Radio plays an important part in helping astronomers find out more about the universe. Objects such as stars and galaxies give out radio waves as well as light. By analyzing these radio waves from space with the help of a computer, astronomers can learn how far away a star is, how hot it is and other facts. These radio signals are often very weak, so astronomers use large dish-antenna receivers to pick them up. Scientists are also looking for radio signals sent by other intelligent life forms. We have sent similar signals from powerful radio transmitters. If there are any "neighbors" in space, radio will be the way in which we first get in touch with them.

▽ This is the world's largest radio telescope, located in Puerto Rico. It is used to pick up faint radio signals from distant stars and galaxies.

Glossary

Amplitude   The amplitude is a measure of a wave's power. It is the distance between the top of the peak of a wave and a line drawn through the middle. As the power of a wave increases, so does its amplitude.

Antenna   A metal rod or wire that is used to transmit and receive radio waves. Dish-shaped antennae are used to pick up and concentrate weak radio signals, or to direct radio waves at orbiting satellites.

Frequency   A wave's frequency is measured by the number of waves that pass a fixed point each second. The higher the frequency is, the more waves per second there are. Different frequencies are used to carry different broadcasts.

Interference   This is the term given to the confusion of radio signals, caused by stray radio waves, or by radio waves of different frequencies affecting each other.

Ionosphere   This is a region of the atmosphere that contains electrically-charged particles. This layer reflects most radio waves back to Earth, enabling us to communicate over long distances. Radio waves of ultrahigh frequency, however, pass straight through the ionosphere, and so we use these to communicate with satellites.

Receiver   This is the electrical equipment that receives radio waves from an antenna and converts them into electrical current. The current is in turn converted to sound in a radio, or into sound and pictures in the case of a television receiver.

Transmitter   A transmitter works in the opposite way to a receiver. It converts electrical currents into radio waves, to be broadcast from an antenna.

Index

A aircraft, 14, 15, 22, 25
airline pilot, 8
airport, 20, 24
ambulance, 8
amplitude, 10
animals, 23
antenna, 8, 11
   cheese, 15
   dish, 13, 14, 27
   telescopic, 11
antimissile system, 24
army, 24
astronomy, 27
atmosphere, 12

B battery, 22
beacon, 22
bicycle, 13
blip, 14
Boeing AWAC, 23
broadcast, 11, 13, 14, 18, 24, 26
business, 18

C car, 18
charting, 16
Citizen's Band radio, 18
   language, 18
communication, 13, 18, 19, 22, 24, 25, 26
computer, 14, 20, 24, 27

E earth, 12, 13, 26
echo, 16
electrical current, 10
   energy, 10
   equipment, 14

F farmer, 20
fighter, 25
fishing vessel, 16
frequency, 10, 11, 13, 14, 24
   ultrahigh, 13

G galaxy, 27

H hydrophone, 16

I interference, 10, 18
ionosphere, 12, 13

J jamming, 24

L light beam, 13

M mast, 10
meteorological office, 20
models, 8
mountain rescue, 18

R radar, 14, 15, 20, 24
radio, 10, 13, 18

broadcast, 13, 14
bugs, 23
speed, 10
waves, 11, 12, 13, 16, 26, 27
reflected wave, 15
reflection, 13, 14, 15
relay station, 12
remote control, 8
rescue service, 22

S satellite, 13, 20, 26
screen, 14, 15, 20
sea, 16, 20
Seawolf, 24
ship, 11, 14, 15, 16, 20, 22
sonar system, 16
sound wave, 10, 16
space shuttle, 26
stars, 27
submarine, 16

T telephone, 19
television, 10, 11, 23
transmitted wave, 15
transmitter, 8, 23
transmitting station, 12
two-way radio, 18

W wavelength, 10
weather, 8, 11, 14, 20, 22

Acknowledgements
The publishers wish to thank the following people who have helped in the preparation of this book:
British Aerospace, British Telecom, Cable & Wireless, Cardiologic, Citizens Band Association, Ferranti, Marconi, Meteorological Office, Ministry of Agriculture Fisheries & Food, Oceanographic Society, Plessey Radio Systems, Rediffusion, RFD Marine Escape Systems, Rockwell International, Royal National Institute for the Blind, Sperry Systems, Thorn-EMI.

Photographic Credits:
Cover: Robert Harding Associates, *title page:* Art Directors Photo Library, page 9: Zefa, page 13: Cable & Wireless, page 14: Zefa, page 17: Sea Fish Industry Authority; Ferranti Computer Systems Ltd, page 18: David Jacobs, page 19: British Telecom; Cable & Wireless, page 21: Meteorological Office, page 23: Bruce Coleman, page 25: Boeing; Rediffusion, page 27: Arecibo Observatory, National Astronomy & Ionosphere Centre.